# WITHERNSEA:
# A SENSE OF PLACE
# A PLACE OF SENSE

# LIMERICKS FOR
# THE LIGHTHOUSE

by : **GODFREY HOLMES**

**NETHERMOOR BOOKS**

**"St. Elphin,"**

**12 North Promenade**

**Withernsea**

**HU19  2DP**

**Telephone : 01964-615258**

*Contact the Author:*
**godfrey.holmes@btinternet.com**

*The full price of any Copy sold will be donated to
the Withernsea Lighthouse Trust. However,
all viewpoints or standpoints expressed in this Verse
are entirely those of the Author – independent of the Trust;
independent of supporters of the Trust.*

**Dedicated**

**to**

**Carolyn & Paul**

\*\*\*\*\*\*\*\*\*\*\*\*\*\*

High above the wild Ocean

A Tower stands;

High above the bustling Promenade

A Tower stands;

High above make-and-take far below

A Tower stands;

And in the distance -

'Neath the sun & moon & stars -

A Tower stands.

\*\*\*\*\*\*\*\*\*\*\*\*\*\*\*\*\*

# THE LIMERICK

IS A POETIC FORM:
POPULARIZED BY THE POET, ARTIST,
HUMOURIST & MUSICIAN

EDWARD LEAR [ 1812-88 ]...

A STRUCTURE OFTEN ASSUMED TO BE HUMOUROUS
OR BAWDY - OR BOTH.

BUT LIMERICKS CAN ALSO BE VERY SERIOUS -

& CAN CERTAINLY SHOW WIT & WISDOM
WITHOUT RESORT TO INDECENCY OR SPITE.

## THE  EXACT FORMAT OF A LIMERICK IS :

***** FIVE LINES - 1,2,3,4,5...   & FIVE LINES ONLY.

***** LINE TWO SHOULD RHYME OR HALF-RHYME
WITH LINE NUMBER ONE -

***** ALSO WITH LINE NUMBER FIVE.

***** EQUALLY, LINES THREE & FOUR
SHOULD RHYME....

***** LINES THREE & FOUR ARE FREQUENTLY  SHORTER
THAN ALL OTHER LINES.

***** OF INTEREST, THERE IS NO REQUIREMENT WHATEVER
FOR A LIMERICK TO START WITH THE  WORDS :
"THERE ONCE WAS A..."

**********

# WITHERNSEA :
# A SENSE OF PLACE
# A PLACE OF SENSE
## Limericks for the Lighthouse

---

A Place with the freshest air ;
An int'resting Place to share !
Where everyone reaches
Nine, ten, sun-kissed  Beaches -
*Read on !  But of Satire beware !*


Wiv once was a new-found-land:
Defined by sea & fine sand...
A Place to remember
From March to December...
Brighton outclassed  - *& more grand ?*

Pilgrims they surely were :
Explorers  -  if you prefer.
With true Viking verve
They held  their nerve :
Nothing would Cave-men deter.

Clay underfoot was quite heavy -
And Parli'ment wanted a Levy.
Some farmsteads were scattered:
Grown grain all that mattered -
When Tourists arrived, in a bevy !

Junes, then, were extremely pleasant
For even the chilliest Peasant
Who *liked* his first Summer ;
[ Past-August much glummer ! ]
*Bread spread with paté of pheasant ?*

Too soon those four months of *cool:*
Ice-patterns that cause folk to drool ;
Harsh test of survival :
So soon post-arrival ;
Abroad only servant or fool.

The Esplanade had to come first
[ And how grumpy Settlers cursed ! ]
When new money arrived
They felt more deprived :
Their lot, Fate decreed, the worst.

Withernsea *did*  get a Railway link:
Bannister's dream laid down in a blink !
Broderick's  fine Station
For day-trip - vacation ? -
Fares Cheaper than most would think.

How Wiv's *first*  Pier was badly battered
[ Ships through its timbers clattered  ]
Full length shrank in stages
[ How storm's anger rages!  ]
Founding dreams so rudely shattered !

In sunshine, *Pier Towers*  are golden :
To Conway their builders beholden.
In all there are four -
Seen right down the Shore :
Enough a *new*  Pier to embolden ?

Long Promenades also were raised :
Their promoters quite unfazed.
They even piped Gas,
Telephones, alas!
[ *Their ingenuity praised*  ]

A stranger must understand
A Lighthouse built far inland !
Standing so tall:
So solid each wall !
Tickets bought on demand.

Magnificent views from the top;
Tourists urged not to flop
After all that clamber -
Kay Kendall's dress amber -
Withernsea's clustered backdrop.

*" Mum : are we half way there ?*
*I can't do another Stair!*
*We've been round and round:*
*So far from the ground !*
*My shoes are beginning to wear...."*

And during past Golden Age
Prized Minstrels did not renege
On their promise to act -
Tossed coins to exact? -
So buoyed on Withernsea's stage !

Showboats swung on the Sands,
Stunts, stilts and contests grand !
All sorts of fun,
Cheap toys to be won !
Outings not ending as planned ?

Bank Holiday Beaches were packed:
*Nearness*  fun-seekers scarce lacked!
They came in their scores:
To *wider* Outdoors !
*[ This Resort had everything cracked ! ]*

Pre-fridge, warmth got to the ices;
For the seller: melting, a crisis.
*" Far safer buy rock*
*Or a new Summer frock ! "*
With children in tow : sacrifices.

Youngsters wore quite formal suits -
Breaches & bonnets cute -
*" Like little grown men " :*
[ No halfway stage then ! ]
Prim grown-ups upholding repute.

Then there were bathers *nude*
Which wasn't considered rude !
They tasted the waters
Away from their daughters!
[ *So rarely afeared of the Prude* ]

Did they *really*  take Switchback  ride ?
Did they free-skate side-to-side ?
What made up their fun
'Neath watery Sun ?
[ Head home - or sodden abide ? ]

Did they *really*  lift up the oar:
Five-foot above blue Lake's new floor ?
How hard  did they paddle
In wood boats to straddle ?
[ How oft was shore's summons ignored ! ]

Did they *really*  see Village Model?
[ Next Mere - where Mallards did waddle ? ]
Each construct so slender !
With mini fire-tender !
Each bairn, each pet, mollycoddle ?

Did they *really*  attend Hollym Races :
Eventing which left so few traces ?
Remarkable cheering
When finish-line nearing !
[ *Punters astride their suitcases!* ]

Did they *really*  play serious Tennis ?
"Set One, 40-love, to Dennis !"
Who owned cat-gut Racquet ?
In Middle-Class bracket ?
*Florins*  to hand - not pennies.

Did they *really*  play crown-green bowls ?
On turf needing soft crèpe soles?
" Where's heading the Jack ? "
" Whose throw shows the knack ? "
[ *A Game not relying on Goals !* ]

And did they *really*  use Pool external?
[ Brisk exercise: natural, eternal   ]
Practising strokes
[ No booze & no smokes !  ]
*Just outclass each slowcoach infernal !*

Did they *really*  get thrown out of lodgings ?
[ Fierce Landladies' rampage wise dodging ? ]
So few coins for spending -
More borrowed : *not lending.*
[ Much make-do & no little codging ? ]

A few day trippers had bikes
[ A few more had invalid trikes  ]
Those days of bone-shaking
[ What risks riders taking ! ]
Or strolling, more to their likes ?

Wiv was built by jobbing Spec-Builder :
Short leases so writ to bewilder !
Or Sale to one's Neighbour
To pay for more labour
[ A Home fit for Alf & Matilda ?  ]

And those Porches ceramically tiled !
[ Function & Art reconciled  ]
A prized North-facing Larder !
[ Stone floors seem much harder !  ]
Pan-Closet: "out-in-the-wild" !

Population speed'ly doubled :
All that brickwork ; all that rubble !
House rows built on spec :
Mixed standards ?  No check ?
[ *Hired joiners joining  the Bubble* ]

Some housing provided *good*  rooming
For people with nemesis looming ?
Caught  by recession ?
[ The Great Depression ? ]
Some quick bucks, or odd jobs, presuming ?

One Street is named after *Cammidge.*
[ Mercifully free of much damage ! ]
He's one of Wiv's founders
[ Not one of life's Bounders  ]
Some gain wealth through prudent marriage !

One Street is named after Cheverton.
[ *P'raps a supporter of Everton ? ]*
He loved the Seaside :
South Prom trim - and wide -
Best seen when all bad weather's gone !

Another road honours James Young
[   Distinguished Townsmen among   ]
It led to Band-Stage
[   Wiv's pre-Streaming age !   ]
Thereon could his praises be sung.

The Street that is named for *a Queen*
Camilla Shand's already seen !
Queen Vic never rode it...
Nor Queen Mary strode it...
*Our Queen*  should really have been !

On one Street that's named after *Walter :*
Where Witnesses have their High Altar ;
And Fire Station best sited
For arsonists blighted ?
Bus drivers nip down, neither falter.

*Intently,* prestige was sought :
*Better folk*  coastward brought ?
But Southport's ambition
Matched Bournemouth's position.
[   Brid's wild card: its Fishing Port   ]

Meanwhile this Town has *a grid* :
Straight streets with few buildings hid.
*Parallel* roads -
Each with Post-Codes.
[ Who visits for *en suite* must bid ! ]

Lost mem-ries: gentle tea-dances ;
Foxtrot, Quickstep... Romances !
Sax-ophonist downbeat ;
Trumpeters *up* beat ;
*Pianists aware of side-glances ?*

'Neath Parasols Ladies would walk -
Hushed tones their earnest talk :
These *not* servant lasses -
But aspirant Classes
[ No squalid conquests to chalk ! ]

Beer: only a couple of pence :
Warm surrounds; atmosphere dense.
Cradling dwindling cup
Till hearing: "Drink Up !"
[ *Another* Inn the where & the whence ]

Some Youths would sleep under tents :
Exhausted savings' extent ?
They ate humble pie :
On coarse mats to lie -
Till back t'wards Bradford they went !

When nobody handled much money :
Deprivation didn't sound funny.
With ends forced to meet -
Despair's cry discreet ?
[ Line slung to catch the odd tunny ]

Penny or tupp'ny machines
Gobbled many-a fun-seekers' means.
Who gained the windfall
[ Glance-favoured pin-ball ? ]
At Sunset saw winnings so lean.

Entertainment rather dull ?
So toffs jigged the more in Hull.
Withernsea down in the dumps ?
[ Wessies not short of grumps ! ]
Empty pockets - but beaches full !

Five Chippies were owned by *Redfern's* :
The gaffer was Len - with sideburns.
They sold, too, wet plaice,
Fried chicken - with taste :
Whilst staff at the range took their turns.

*Jackson's:* the Grocer old-fashioned
Served shoppers quite quiet - or passioned.
Their Store at the Junction
Displayed no compunction
Selling Bacon so recently rationed.

*Frost's* sold so much fresh fruit ;
Spuds, parsnips, beans, beetroot.
Eggs by the Dozen
[ A treat for your Cousin ! ]
And Partridges shot in the shoot.

Where once folk enjoyed late-night clubbing:
Prized promont'ry site took a drubbing :
Sun Terrace with boarding
[ No Pirates marauding ! ]
*Now young'uns go more for Hull-Pubbing.*

On the Beach they have high wind-shields
For North Wind which sharp cutlass wields.
*" Put on that tweed jacket ! "*
*" Flat cap: did you pack it ? "*
*" To think:  once our raincoats we peeled ! "*


And on each Bonfire Night
The skies are with rockets alight.
Just look at the blaze !
[ Midst No-vember's haze ! ]
*" Finale" is still the best sight !*

And *when*  Christmas Lights are switched on :
The Old Year so ruefully gone ?
Just hear the loud cheers
When Santa appears !
Street-sellers by Lamp-posts outshone.

And *if*  you've promptly inquired -
And *if*  you're prop'ly attired :
From Social Club [ Boating  ]
You'll come out gloating...
[ Members : *No Boat required* !  ]

Glasshouses look rather bare:
Few plants or shrubs flourish there.
No Alpines, no heather,
No Chrysanths to weather ?
Green skills less ready to share ?

The *fields* are adorned with ripe Rape :
Bright yellow making folks gape !
Of all English flowering,
*This* most o'erpowering...
*No need in the future to vape !*

Summer brings Elvis pretenders:
Silk-suited - with woven suspenders.
Cliff, Bruce, Stevie, Cilla :
Scores true to scintilla !
[ Each Tribute great following renders ]

*" Yes: it's '* Presley *' I'm wanting to meet :*
*In* Valley Gardens to greet.
*He knows every word ;*
*Wears costume absurd ?*
*To* Gracelands *he now retreats ! "*

19

*Which tribute compels  you  to stand :*
*On Stage, in front of the Band ?*
*Is it Barry ?  Is it Roy ?*
*[ Rolling Stone : greater  joy ?  ]*
*Some music : live, some canned.*

We also have young baton-holders :
Earning their high-mark grade folders.
They twist & they twirl,
Clutched flags to unfurl :
Shy girls :  each Performance much bolder.

Girl *dancers*  have dance-practice weekly :
" *Move swifter !* "  " *Inherit space meekly !* "
Hip-hop - or tango ;
Red costumes - or mango.
[ Ballet *out of doors*  tackled sleekly  ]

Verity-Lee runs *her own*  School of Dancing :
Imperfect routines never chancing.
She asks girls for sequence :
Deft moves born of frequence.
*[ Guys: don't think they're only prancing ! ]*

And what of the pedal-bike ?
[ In Towns most cyclists like ]
Why not join a Club ?
[ Yorkshire's quite a bike hub ! ]
Mid-road still  better than dyke !

When Withernsea's part of *Le Tour*
Top Cyclists may pass your front door :
The fastest in yellow:
*Superior*  fellow !
[ Some backsides by saddle made sore ]

And when youth take to the saddle
Challenge will not their wits addle !
They'll need some persistence -
Mounts without assistance ? -
" Who'll rate pedal over *paddle  ?* "

Withernsea also has *horses*
Whose speed no one enforces :
Let loose on the sand,
Their gallop so grand...
Which gives us horses for courses !

Each day observe a brown Spaniel:
His Biblical name is *Daniel.*
He gives folk great joy :
Slather ! Annoy !
And siring this Pup is *Nathaniel.*

Some homes keep hounds and Alsatians...
Pugs, bull-dogs  - or spotted Dalmatians ?
See poodles cross-bred,
And collies well-fed...
*Jack Russells*  : one priest's appellation.

Of *cats*  our streets have but few :
Seen sometimes: a kitten new !
They're generally wary :
Of dogs they feel scary !
*Give each Ginger Tom his due.*

*Most*  homes keep the sea-gulls at bay :
Those vultures with heads white and grey...
Who flee for their lives,
Then feed their good wives :
*Not really bad birds of prey ?*

*Do not make our sea-gulls too tame*
*[ These scavengers get a bad name !  ]*
*They'll swoop on your cornet,*
*Buzz past like a hornet.*
*[ Nicked sandwich no cause for shame !  ]*

Withernsea has but a dozen cows :
Whatever farm finance allows.
Instead we have wheat -
And some sugar-beet...
So milk-stools give way to the plough.

And where are those fields full of sheep ?
Where do those little lambs peep ?
Our Shepherds are few -
Saved for barley crops new -
Farm Subsidies in pockets deep ?

At *Northfield :* an Organ Society !
[ Piped music of hugest variety ! ]
Jazz, Film, Op'ra, Symphony
On Keyboard - with Timpani !
Tunes *spiritual*  nurture their Piety.

Wiv *does* have an Army platoon :
For camouflaged youngsters, a boon !
Cadets find a hobby
[ All clear of the Bobby ! ]
Conscription will come all too soon ?

Footy's *part* of each Sunday's ritual :
Played  best before plated victuals !
Dads & Lads do the shouting.
Visiting Teams like the outing ?
*[ Blaming the Ref : habitual ! ]*

*Your team: it appears on your shirt ;*
*If SPURS:  that is bound to hurt.*
*Why not back MAN.CITY ?*
*[ You'll never face pity ! ]*
*Or with SCUNTHORPE you might flirt.*

*Our Golf Course is par Seventy-Two:*
*Best done when your worst shots are few !*
*You'll go out in forty;*
*Less back - if you're naughty !*
*Each Member knows you through and*
*through.*

When thirsty, folk *first use* *"The Pier "*;
Then try *"The Commercial "* [ austere ? ]....
Move on to "The Station" -
Then feel much elation :
*"The Plough "* serves a perfect guest beer.

Pass by our "new" *Lifeboat  Station:*
Affirming unpaid dedication !
Light, fast, rubber dinghy
[ Some donors so mingy ! ]
Those rescued : filled with elation ?

Our Town boasts a new *Policing*  Station:
Cause of great Expectation.
They'll catch all those Thieves !
And grant no Reprieves !
What gives rogues their motivation ?

Don't miss Wiv's War-Mem-orials :
Hushed sites of silence Mayorial.
[ Remembering each Hero
Whose future proved Zero
In Trenches whose stench was corporeal  ]

On Proms you turn Left or Right:
1-80 degrees  in your sight.
Instead of three-sixty
[ With Valleys betwixt ye  ]
Go boldly into the Night !

On South Prom: a big private boatyard
For Skippers who know they must sail hard.
They mend, scour & varnish
Each rail that might tarnish ;
Upturned, there's a hull to be tarred !

The fountains: they're playing up high ;
They might even reach your thigh !
They've got them in Hull !
So life's never dull.
Let's hope they their critics defy.

The *end* of South Promenade:
Appears on an old Postcard.
It hasn't changed much :
Since founding plans such.
[ *Though newer homes sometimes jarred*  ]

Spot magnificent Billboards [ twenty ? ]
Engage passers-by aplenty.
In stark black-&-white:
An historian's *delight !*
Nostalgia, regret, as blent be.


" *Is it safe to stand in the Ocean?* "
" *Yes - if you apply Sun Lotion.*"
" *Your spotted bikini*
*Is daringly weeny !* "
" *Sand games : for ills the best potion !* "


Folk love to go step-counting each :
Descending with bliss to the beach.
Or *up*  one-by-one
To catch setting Sun.
" *On stairs you might Heaven reach !* "


" *Can you pass my bucket & spade ?* "
" *Do I crawl on my tummy - or wade ?* "
"*On each hottest day*
*On the beach I will play* "
[ *Of such fun are pastimes made* ]

Some days we're afraid of high waves :
Great fun - or a watery grave ?
Davy-Jones' locker :
Still comes as shocker
To they whom no life-belt can save.

The nearness of drowning's so real
Yet Tempest's excitement we feel!
Mortality's waiting -
The storm now abating -
*Neptune's cull - with no appeal.*

When waves aren't so fierce and so high -
No spray rising right up to the sky ! -
Seals swim quite near :
Their playful pups dear !,
Heading back South, by and by.

On still Sea, folk lie out flat
[ Each like a wind-blown hat ? ]
" *What joy now to float :*
*I could be a boat ! "*
....If not in " Old Boatshed " sat !

The lads swim in Lycra trunks :
Lasses all loving these hunks !
Or plain pants they wear -
When sent in for a dare
[ Like biscuits all out for the dunk  ]

Forbidden to ride a Skateboard
[ Upsetting frail neighb'ly accord ? ]
Rollerblades too -
Even Segways *few....*
Forbidden to break from the hordes ?

*Kayaks*  have replaced Canoes :
For paddling, if you so choose.
It's very exciting:
Beating sand-kiting...
*" If sea-sick, just keep off the booze ! "*

We're left with a single Mere :
Deeper than first appears.
It's open for fishing...
For passers-by wishing
They'd paid for some snork'lling gear.

One Angler competes for his prize:
On hook, line & rod Rod relies.
A two-kilo cod !
[ Thanksgiving to God ! ]
Best bait was a dangled surprise !

Offshore are a great deal of Crab
[ Washed, dressed: their taste is ab fab ! ]
They're caught in wood cages
[ Full growth may take ages ]
*" And now you must fillet your Dab ! "*

Wind *turbines* stand out in the deep :
Energy costs downwards to keep....
Their huge blades go round :
Not making a sound ?
*" Climb ladder - and have a peep ! "*

Day-break on a Winter morning :
Runners running - but, weary, yawning.
*Daily Mails* on Sale :
Good read - without fail ?
Is front page uplift - or a warning ?

Our Prom draws a blanket of fog
*[ " No sight of you on your jog ! " ]*
So take a strong lamp
To shine on the ramp....
*" And borrow your neighbour's Guide Dog ! "*

*Is that  Flamborough  that we see?*
*[ Fine headland, you'll agree ! ]*
*Flamborough's beams add to four;*
*Take four breaths, four more....*
*Night-time's  infinity !*

*" In Withernsea's  harshest  December :*
*' Tis East Wind you'll most remember !*
*Each  Northerly  blast*
*Will leave you aghast...*
*Till following 1st. of September ! "*

*" You're buying a Dormobile ?*
*Your bed behind steering-wheel ! "*
*Sleeping at kerbside:*
*From locals best hide !*
*Your breakfast no seagull must steal ! "*

For fifty weeks of the year
*Hell's Angels* come not here.
They travel elsewhere
In search of fresh air -
Lest Vespas should re-appear !

Each trundling mobility scooter
Is fitted with unused hooter.
Will *you* be flattened ?
[ A.& E. fattened? ]
Who's needing a Penalty Shooter ?

*" Beware broken glass in the street ;*
*Or hid in sand 'neath young feet ?*
*Glass gives us clear sight -*
*And drinks, to delight....*
*Yet misplaced : its harm is complete."*

Wiv still has six curio dealers :
Twixt Chemist Shops staffed by healers.
Gems, antiques & junk -
Loot not to debunk !
[ Oak pews, stained glass, & kneelers ]

"Give to *Gateway !* "- some folk are told -
*"And bring in whate'er can be sold ! "*
Don't trust the Car Boot
But in attics root
For tools or Silver or Gold.


Posh clothing makes *Dove House* good cash:
Clothing pre-loved - or rash !
Plus discarded Games
With forsaken names !
*Dove House has no house-room for trash.*


The *LIONS* will sell you electrics-
And Carpet Squares pre-metric !
They do draw keen browsers
[ In Shorts - or flared trousers! ]
*New babies require the obstetric !*


*Heron's* our Grocer local :
Its staunchest custom quite vocal ;
Its prices most reasonable
[ Defection quite treasonable ! ]
Compare each pack ; ask each Yokel.

*" At Poundstretch, we'll buy for our Party :*
*Each plateful will look very arty !*
*In a field near to Tesco*
*We'll eat all-alfresco...*
*The parson, replete, hale and hearty ! "*

*ALDI's* reach has remarkably grown :
Low prices not hitherto known !
The items folk favour
Are sweet - with no flavour :
From distant aerodromes flown !

*ALDI* has a *middle* Aisle :
Assorted goods in a pile.
They're not this time edible :
Some bargains incredible.
*Our shopping might take quite a while !*

*Tesco* was quite a late-comer
To brighten each shopper's Summer.
Built on a Siding
It soon took a hiding
From *Proudfoot's* owner glummer.

*You* might *want a few Souvenirs:*
*How your day at the Seaside appears ?*
A pretty tea-towel ?
*Glazed gull - or lace owl ?*
*Fridge-magnets & cups full of cheer.*

*" Where can we buy some ice-cream ? "*
*" Without it, our babe will scream ! "*
*" Best try local makes ! "*
*" Whipped cornets - with Flakes ? "*
*[ Some flavours truly off-beam ]*

Wiv's Post Office serves lots of senders ;
Notes dished out to folk on their benders.
Some parcels returning
To warehouses churning
More packets for agents & lenders.

Wiv *used to* have three good Banks
Where folks' spare cash - not much ! - sank.
Trippers *do* like real money
[ Direct Debit seems funny ? ]
*And the chimney pot's rather dank !*

One Caff has its pre-Season clients -
On Bac'n-&-Eggs quite reliant.
They all love the chatter
Till 5 - when they scatter!
[ *Their sausages lean, fat - or giant ! ]*

*Munching that fresh currant scone*
*[ A little more soft than your phone ! ]*
*Press each of its buttons*
*[ Gulp down like a glutton ? ]*
*And now it's your dog's favoured bone !*

Of "Instant" be duly tight-lipped:
Just like brown hot water when sipped ?
But with *strong* roast coffee
Buy cake made of toffee,
And ask for your milk to be whipped.

Queen Street  *has good places to eat*
*If you don't want to eat on a seat.*
*" Pavlova rice ? "*
*" Plum crumble is nice ! "*
*"...And  do  have some veg. with your meat."*

Past Midnight a Pizza queue :
Sent also to fetch some lamb stew.
On a plateful of spuds :
"Those kebabs  look duds ! "
*"And when are the Noodles due ? "*

Does our Town value home cooking ?
For saucepans are residents looking ?
Or do they prefer
*This*  chore to defer ....
And ring to secure Table Booking ?

*Markets*  belong to the past ?
[ Rather too makeshift to last ?  ]
We do have one  stall :
Outside, near the wall.
*Their flowers sell really fast !*

On high street, pass two high street bookies :
Attracting some high-rolling rookies.
Whatever the horse -
[ Fifth back o'er the Course ? ]
Yields stale crust instead of rich cookies !

*You can then bet on League Cup Winners :*
*On Forwards : in Sin-bins the Sinners ?*
*Who'll get a Nil Draw ?*
*Score two goals - or four ?*
*[ Life's rarely a stream of free Dinners ]*

Bingo promises, too, greater riches
*[ The Caller will have you in stitches ! ]*
" Sweet Seventy-Seven:
*Get ready for Heaven ! "*
Your Card - very tempting - bewitches.

In Arcades folk spend their shillings :
*To lose all* these Punters seem willing !
Slots hungry they choose,
Four fruits to peruse :
New gamblers with coin tubs round milling.

Coin-sweeps are by far most deceptive -
· Of ten-pees inviting, receptive.
The next heap will fall
Once you've given your all :
*Fools' judgment most keenly perceptive ?*

*" And never need you  spend one pound :*
*Just keep walking round and around !*
*Watch the grieving of others -*
*Their stakes to recover ?*
*[ Their weeping  not making a sound !  ] "*


The Dodgems cry out for side-crashing  :
Their Circuit prepared for the bashing !
*Pretend it's stock-racing -*
*Disaster embracing  -*
Past log-jams eagerly dashing.


*" Once a year at the Travelling Fair*
*Go skyward : strapped to a chair !*
*Then hook plastic duck ;*
*With slings try your luck ?*
*For tilting tea-cups prepare !  "*


Don't miss Wiv's Carnival Procession :
Of Route it takes full possession.
Wear Pirates' striped clothing
[ Their worst heists still loathing ]
*Or dress as a Priest for Confession !*

The *Pav's* got a huge Deck-Chair :
Get seated thereon - if you dare !
What a great photo opp !
What a fine pageant prop !
Gymnasts only stop and stare !

And what of *Pavilion's* flume :
So fast, you're sent to your doom ?
Round twisting bends
Your body wends:
Custom hitting a boom !

With religion some people grapple :
Helped on at a Wesleyan Chapel.
'Twas pride of Queen Street :
Its lead Spire so neat !
Brought down like a windfall apple.

Its Sister on *Hull Road's* Right-hand -
Azure oval Balcony grand -
Deems Preaching central ....
With prayers penitential ;
*Tuesday's " Flavours " best food in the land !*

Wiv's largest [ Civic ] Church
Is locked : leaving brides in the lurch ?
*Will it become Apartments ? -*
*Exhibition compartments ? -*
*Or falconry's unhindered perch ?*

Further t'wards Hull is *St. Matt's -*
Where worshippers sit for a chat.
It stages good Drama -
Artistic  panoramas -
Chants Mary's *Magnificat.*

For those who've crossed over to Rome,
Rome has come closer to home !
Cath'lics meet near Bus Garage -
The Pope : don't disparage !
*But all your Scriptures comb.*

Forget not the PresbyCongs :
Their texts & their cheerful songs.
They meet to the South
Intercessions to mouth...
And each foll'wer for *Unity*  longs.

Await just 7-30 days
To join in two *Passion* Plays :
Three Crosses 'neath blue skies -
A Master even Peter denies -
Easter's Story to-excite & amaze.

*" Have you noticed how one  Store's trolleys*
*Augment many a front yard's follies ?*
*Have they been  taken ?*
*For Bath-chairs mistaken ?*
*Some folk even pinch their Pub's brollies ! "*

Whatever - you ask - is much sadder
Than a builder without his steel ladder?
He left it one day -
While cleaning sea spray....
*And now it's with owner much badder !*

Some gardens are hoisting a flag:
Their loyalties  oft-times to brag.
Will the Tricolour flutter ?
*" St George ! "* you might mutter.
*[ Don't try an Old Soldier to gag! ]*

Life can be so horribly cruel -
When cars can't take on more fuel !
Our one Petrol Station
Has odd aberration :
Deliveries needing renewal.

*The Library* hands out advice
On bins, drains, evictions - lice.
Girls go there for Shelter,
Their Mums with a welter
Of crises to make you blink twice.

Withernsea depends on its *Lettings:*
Flats abundant in such pleasant settings.
Rents perforce kept "low" :
Each void, a struck blow....
[ Landlords absent: absent, too, any vetting ]

And if it's a *Computer* you need,
Strict user-rules best that you heed !
More pages on screen
For deft surfers keen...
*Keep Googling; to Twitter be keyed !*

And if it's *your M.P.* you seek out:
Status won't cause you to freak out.
He'll hear all your tales
[ Of Council which fails? ]
Whilst urging long-sufferers to speak out.

Councillors stand, too, on the street :
Knowing not whom they will meet.
Folk come with their queries
[ Not political theories ]
Will *new* nerds 'gainst them compete ?

*Most passers-by greet you with relish:*
*Their news to convey - or embellish.*
*Happ'ly, few take the hump*
*[ View you as mugwump ? ]*
*Shunned Goodwill can feel awful Hellish !*

Wiv Bus-drivers always smile;
They smile for mile after mile.
They face tough congestion,
Which harms their digestion.
*They'll drop you down next a stile !*

Young girls on the Bus are excited :
Their natural good humour ignited.
The sound of their chatter
[ Relationships matter ! ]
Stops only when tired you've alighted.

With *Tablets* they're tot'lly engrossed :
Each new photo aiming to post.
It's called "Social Media" :
[ Beyond *Wikipedia* ]
Of "Friends" by the dozen to boast.

*An hour-long phone-call's arresting;*
*To privacy's absence attesting!*
*How cheeky to track*
*Its course fro-and-back!*
*Eavesdroppers are rarely protesting!*

Wiv's lasses dress just as they please -
Tight jeans with a tear at the knees -
Quite daring tank-tops,
*Doc Martens, flip-flops ;*
*Bronze brassieres twanged for a tease.*

Observe boys' clothes *out of School* :
They all look so dapper - so cool !
Their waistcoats so tight ;
Their footwear so light !
*Some show-offs, some playing the Fool !*

A lad sits with chips in a shelter :
His Girlfriend, next-to, a real belter!
While he does her kiss,
Her fish goes amiss.
*[ A poor take-away has he dealt her! ]*

Some fam'lies you'll find are "blended" :
Especially where marriage has ended.
New sisters and brothers -
"Significant Others" -
Where kinship's ties torn go unmended.

Withernsea scholars:  *so polite!*
[   After breakfast, then at night ]
Their behaviour a marker
[ Adolescence less darker?  ]
Good teachers taught them aright !

*Withernsea High School* was a trial :
"11-plus" failure's denial....
Rurality's best learning ;
Fine teaching turning
Non-starters to Uni, awhile.

To College Wiv's scholars repair :
Learn woodwork, plumbing - or hair ;
Or choose dental nursing
[ Their lips tightly pursing ? ]
*Most pressing : there's Elderly Care !*

Wiv does have its local Gazette:
*Reporters reporting : you bet !*
This Town on a high
Can reach for the Sky !
Good News is half what we get.

We hear, too, of *wickedest* deeds :
Drunkenness, fraud and greed ;
Brash youths simply foolish
[ Some Readers quite ghoulish? ]
*For justice does this organ plead.*

A Cottage Hospital once stood at Queen's
[ Healed pensioners more than teens ]
Valued treatment giving
To those struggling living :
Three Infirm'ries in between.

*Still open from eight until eight ??*
[ Should Injury come not too late? ]
*We must have recourse -*
With no other source
Of help when we're in a bad state.

Our Railway fell to Lord Beeching
[ Ignoring our earnest beseeching ]
On board was a Guard
Whom closure hit hard :
*His train no more villages reaching.*

Through Caravans row-upon-row
Could *Withernsea's* tourism grow ?
Some towed to chosen pitch ;
Some owned by campers rich ?
Will developers more spaces bestow ?

Big trailers arrive on low-loaders ;
Their owners in fancy off-roaders ?
They have lots of rooms,
Mod-cons one assumes ?
And the Loo: it leaves no bad odour.

*Mobile Homes  :* they have many names,
On Sites full of fun and games.
They're not really temp'rary :
Their insides exemplary.
*Just heed lest one goes up in flames !*

All Caravans seek a good *Club  :*
Selling whisky & home-made grub.
Then there's Comedy Night,
And a Quiz-master bright !
*Provided you've kept up your Sub.*

*Our Static's now let to Miranda :*
*So plush, with an ample Verandah !*
*Incredibly spacious....*
*[ Its Site fees : voracious ! ]*
*When losing the plot, don't meander !*

*That Bungalow's all made of wood :*
*Sawn planks either rotten or good.*
*Outside : a deck-chair*
*[ A world without Care ! ]*
*Loose living as best understood.*

*"Seathorne  " was built* in the Eighties :
Retired folk finding new maties !
They live as they choose ;
Play Bridge : win or lose...
And eat sausage pie with some taties !

At *Rimswell : a Tower for clean water*
[ Not seen it ? You really oughta ! ]
A fine circle white -
Its pillars upright :
*Preceding the water transporter.*

At *Halsham :* a stark Mausoleum -
For vespers, lament & *Te Deum.*
Constables laid resting :
Their standing attesting.
*Past Midnight: imagine you see  em !*

*Hilston's* Church is very recent:
Stock design, extremely decent.
Re-built for three score :
With sturdy oak door.
*[ German bombers : how malfeasant! ]*

At *Waxholme*, they have an old Mill :
Solid and ivy-clad, still.
Would suit Restoration :
A four-bed creation ?
[ If builders just had the skill ! ]

Now for the Holderness *"Queen"* ...
From Spurn Head distant seen !
*St. Patrick's* has beauty ;
To its village a duty
To welcome the humble & mean.

*Patrington's* dreaming Spire
*Inspires* its resident Choir....
An elegant building
Of stonework and gilding :
*The Holy Spirit on fire!*

*Patrington* still boasts *a beacon*
[ Prim. Chapel served by a Deacon ]
Just beyond : a Cricket Ground
[ At *their* Mill : a Jump-Course found ! ]
With Horse-Chestnuts, shall we find Pecan ?

To-day : bored class sent to *Garton*
[ Considerably nearer than *Barton* ! ]
They'll go via *Roos* -
Skirt ditches and sluice -
And buy milk in little square cartons.

*Keyingham's* Church lost its Spire :
[ Its internal structure dire ? ]
Yet keeps a stone  tower-
Seen past yonder bower -
*Maybe that's all bats require ?*

At *Mappleton* live many swine :
That folk at High Table might dine.
They share a big shed -
No straw for a bed -
*Their numbers may soon see decline.*

In *Withernwick*, see many foals :
In a field shared with a few moles.
They look so new-born -
Their hooves not well-worn -
But soon they will jump over Poles.

At *Welwick* they recall the Plot :
Gunpowder that might kill the lot !
Were its schemers disloyal ?
[ Fit to dip in hot oil? ]
*Dig for gravel ; for victory not !*

*Holmpton's Bunker is famous*
*[ No Cold War allowed to shame us ] :*
*Did Churchill live there ?*
*Or Hull's ex-Lord Mayor ?*
*Four minute warning enough to tame us ?*

At *Easington* they import raw fuel
[ The North Sea : not always cruel ]
All its Pipelines are policed :
By ten coppers, at least !
Single Gas tariffs - or dual ?

At *Kilnsea,* a Twitcher's near *Spurn :*
That home of the Redwing & Tern....
A past Army base
Fortified in case
Nazis invade - slash & burn.

*Spurn* hosts Pilots - also explorers -
Conservationists whose terrain if porous -
Between North Sea & Humber :
Shells, fossils, *without number.*
"Desert Island" alert to Dawn Chorus.

*Aldbrough :* 20 miles up the Coast....
*Camp there - where Sun shines the most !*
"Tis a very diff'rent destination :
Stage in longer peregrination ? ....
Where Painter to Subject gets close..

*Burstwick's* where people make putts :
A Dormitory Village with guts.
It still feels quite rural...
With Clubs in the plural...
Peaceful when everything shuts ?

*" Each Wednesday : Hedon Market.*
*Bob took the car - but couldn't park it !*
*So he drove on to Swine:*
*There bought some white wine...*
*A bell tolled - but he couldn't hark it."*


The *Co-op* in *Hedon* is small -
But meets folk's requirements all.
If they travel to *Thorn*,
Their nerves get more worn -
*But Cash comes straight out the wall !*


*Augustine   remains Hedon's* Saint
[ Let nothing his memory taint ]
His Church - more an Abbey -
Is known to each Cabbie....
He heals each inner complaint.


For *Hornsea Pott'ry* : a house of its own -
Oh how its Collection has grown !
A wondrous reminder
Of decades much kinder
To designers beforehand unknown.

*Hornsea :* home of old motor-cars
Which no Council-on-Earth would debar.
Faced with this traffic -
*Local traders seraphic ?* -
Day-trippers head there from afar.

*Hornsea* now has brand new *bandstand*
Where gymnasts can practise their
handstand.
It's near those two *lions* -
Two manes folk may try on ? -
Before mounting yon yachting Grandstand !

*Hornsea did*  have a Railway Station :
Joseph Wade's inspired inspiration.
For years left to rot -
Grand archways forgot -
*In such a central location.*

*Burton Constable  :* Hull's Stately Manor -
Its dynasty blazed on banner -
Boasting movers & shakers,
Skilled cabinet-makers.
*Gain entry : all for a Tenner !*

Hull's *Maritime*  Museum is swish
For those who the Oceans do fish.
A Hist'ry of Navigation :
Sails, ships ...Exploration !
[ More  Dockyards about to va-nish ? ]

The *Ferens*  is full of fine Art -
Where ev'ryone's journeys can start.
Sculptures intriguing
[ Galleries fatiguing ?  ]
" *See the Triptych before you depart!* "

One morning spend in "*Street Life* " :
Hull's record of noise and of strife.
See trolleys and trams,
Bath-chairs and prams.
Progress spread out with a knife.

Then wander down *Whitefriar Gate:*
Large shops, old pubs, so ornate.
It's an interesting walk
To dockland's last baulk...
A passage to celebrate !

Hull's got a few Bridges swinging :
Dutch trippers their praises singing !
Barges pass underneath -
Not coming to grief -
*Wide open more lock-gates be flinging !*

Victoria  stands in her Square
[ Enjoying publicity's glare ? ]
Her stamp's universal :
An Empire's dispersal ?
What *King*  any better? -  declare !

Past *Wincolmlee*, the River narrows :
Men repairing traps and harrows.
It's a quaint little maze :
Well worth searcher's gaze !
And allotments  grow all folk's marrows !

*House of Fraser*  condemned  to close :
As *Hammond's* , the place shoppers chose.
These big, varied, stores
Led to dropping of jaws !
Trade now to *St. Stephen's*  oft goes.

Some liked the old *C. & A.:*
Tasteful fashion - with little to pay.
*Sports Direct* is now trading
Posh jeans, tops with braiding.
*[ Watch workers determined to play ! ]*

Hull's *Guildhall* is very plush !
[ Its splendour makes visitors blush ]
Solid oak chairs
For Worshipful Mayors....
*" Council's in Session : Hush ! "*

Males turn, for relief, underground:
With only a tinkle as sound.
What feet trod before !
[ What baggage they bore ! ]
*Theatre's flush in-the-round.*

*City Hall 's* tuneful Musicians
Depend on good Sound Technicians.
Each fine Concert work
Comes as a perk
To each wealthy Artist Patrician.

The *Hall* also hosts Graduation :
[ Degrees met with much adulation ]
And upmarket Weddings
[ Singlehood shedding ]
*And Trade Fairs beyond estimation.*

The *Truck* continues its showing
Of Shows whose Ratings are glowing :
Many experimental ;
Others experiential.
Credit on Playwrights bestowing.

*Year of Culture 's* colour was blue
[ Not dark - but a lighter hue ]
Those Volunt'ry Hosts -
At each feast the Ghosts?-
Never said they hadn't a clue !

*Hull Minster 's* been much swopped round :
Religion part-filling the ground.
Therein many shows...
*God saying : " how goes ? "*
To priests who these precincts do pound.

In *Minster* : beyond the Nave
Are Mem'ries this City must save :
The loss of the *Gaul* -
Its Crew one and all -
Were ever there seamen so brave ?

In shipbuilding's driest dock :
Please turn not to study the clock.
Performers here stage
Works straight from the page....
*Any late-comers : "Knock ! knock!"*

On one renowned landing-stage
Came ferries of *former* age :
From *New Holland* sailing -
Their engines not failing -
Lincolnshire's businessmen sage.

Each night at Marfleet's staithe
You'll come more Seamen to wave
Out on their sailing
To Bruges - with mailings -
P&O's Liner suave.

Old Inn on the front *: The Minerva*
*[ Each rustic lass so proud to serve yer! ]*
Has keg beers eleven :
CAMRA's seventh Heaven !
*[ " Big Order : please don't unnerve her ! " ]*

Tramps thought one morn dawned *brighter* -
Their burdens growing lighter -
So they went to Hull's *jail :*
Its walls did they scale -
And now they'll be sleeping much tighter !

To Hull remanded till Trial
Are convicts convinced of denial.
The Judge in his ermine
Does not speak of "vermin" :
That being *The Sun's* usual style.

Each day Students travel to work :
Zero-hours - where they're driven berserk !
Some live in the Sticks -
Like hens with five chicks ! -
Grudged tips their solitary perk.

More Students go on *to the Venn* -
In *Willoughby*  taught now & then.
*Brynmoor Jones*  holds their books,
In *Middleton*  : good cooks !
And the *Union*  shop sells ev'ry pen !

*MethSoc*  is just one Society
Students join of infinite variety.
*Trinity*  hosts a Squash -
Dress not too  posh ! -
*At least they'll be taught sobriety !*

On Graduates does Hull much depend ?
[  On their Campus each year to descend ]
They help our Economy -
Displaying autonomy -
*You'll meet them round every bend !*

Its forty statues *give*  Hull a boost :
Monuments where pigeons roost !
All types of Memorial :
Each an instant Tutorial.
How Sculptors sculpt when loosed!

And now to avoid  confusion :
This Book must reach *a Conclusion.*
Wiv *has*  Sense of Place,
Good living - and space !
So Poetry's not an Intrusion !

Yet  keep on writing Verse
*[ Rhyme-patterns sometimes a curse ! ]*
Wiv's full of material :
[ Hard-edged - or ethereal  ]
*Imagining seeks not its purse.*

And while we're discussing an Ending
[ Wiv's feeble critics transcending...]
We'll find *Place of Sense*
With virtues immense...
Its High Tide, no need of defending.

So now at close of the Eve :
You *too*  must cheer - *and believe !*
.....Wiv increasingly  boasting
Achievements worth toasting....
Erstwhile happenings retrieve.

\*\*\*\*\*\*\*\*\*\*\*\*\*

# APPENDIX :

## AN ALTERNATIVE ENDING ?

---

**WHAT WOULD HAPPEN IF *SOME* READERS -**

**MAYBE ONLY A FEW ? -**

**HELD A VISION**

**OF NO WITHERNSEA :**

**A GHOST-TOWN WITHERNSEA....**

***DYSTOPIA ?***

---

*read on :*

An enormous Tidal Wave -
As mighty as is grave -
Sweeps o'er our streets :
Great panic ; retreats !
[ No medals for the brave ]

The Ocean comes at speed :
No barriers will it heed.
Withernsea trapped , surely drowned ,
Encompassed by creepy sound !
Exactly as Nature decreed ?

Dads lack the borrowed time
To escape the awful slime.
They gasp in despair ;
[ Rooves be-yond repair! ]
Entombed in grimmest grime.

Babes lie sick in their cots ;
Mums still washing the pots ;
Girls confused in their gardens
Heedless of Fate - which  hardens !
[ Pets wholly helpless : lots ]

Car engines will not start ;
No buses are staffed to depart.
Cycles stand gaunt in their sheds
[ Cyclists down alleyways fled ? ]
No borrowing of farmer's cart !

Two taxis are still stuck in Hull :
With gas contractors full....
They unsuspecting -
Wiv needs protecting.
[ Lift only for herring gull ! ]

News : five sons sit on roof !
Lost neighbours  [ hiding ? ] aloof :
They thanking a hatch
With ease-giving latch.
Survival : the ultimate proof.

Two dozen or so reach the park
Their prospects yet terribly stark :
Trapped in  swilling swell
[ Storms nothing can quell ]
Sky above them : forbiddingly dark !

And then come streaks of lightning ;
Thunder following : so loud & so fright'ning.
Not seen, heard, before : .
[ Folk shook to the core ]
Nor sign of Noon's twilight bright'ning.

A few- very few - run to Roos
Like horses freed : on the loose !
There exiles feel safe :
Mayor placed next to waif !
[ Still dreading the Ocean's whoosh ]

Some Teens reach Water Tower -
Coats shed : to give them more power.
They dare not look back
The foe on their track ?
'Neath many trees'-growth to cower.

In Boatyard's recent arrival :
Chance air-pocket's aiding survival :
Helmsmen locked below deck
Of craft - now a wreck ? -
Recall Wiv's fishing revival.

And what of those missing landlords
Whom no one - drifting - applauds ?
Who ploughed ill-got money
Then reaped Milk-&-Honey :
Now forfeit their ill-got rewards.

The Church was already boarded :
St. Nicholas no longer lauded ?
A Resort freed from God ?
Giving Mammon the nod ?
Satan due honour accorded.

Upstream : a Swimming Pool drained....
Swimmers stark naked & pained ;
No lifting great weights ;
No chatting up Dates.
[Fitness schedules: *torn-up-* or stained]

Meridian's doors  stay shut :
Their film-shows abruptly cut.
No need for Town Meetings -
No Guests needing seating -
No grievance vented: "Tut-tut!"

The Comp now lacks Scholars :
No miscreants to collar!
No Classes to teach -
Nor Targets to reach:
Guide-books that nobody foll-ers.

Most caravans tilt, rudely shattered :
Rent income all that mattered ?
Their power-supply suspended....
Their holiday plans upended....
Loosened doorways battered.

And SHORES which graced Wiv's Prom
Now offers no hand -nor aplomb.
Where folk brought their worries ;
Broke bread; sampled curries !
[ That wave: more destructive than Bomb ]

Fountains once dearly sunk -
In setts, for kids [ no drunks ! ]
Will never rise  a-gain
Nor grown-ups entertain...
Another piece of junk.

TESCO fastens tight its doors
[ Rivals jeer - but no guffaws ]
Its vast Stock will perish.
Past purchases cherish !
Was ever a longer P-A-U-S-E ?

See Boots remain metal-shuttered :
Hopes of cures, unneeded, not uttered.
Queen Street with no traffic!
[ Nor snarl-ups:  once graphic! ]
Wiv, croaking,  scarcely  spluttered.

ALDI holds one "Last Day" SALE -
Footfall falling: bound to fail -
And only ONE Assistant
[ Her "Offers" persistent ! ]
From Goole, she missing gale.

County Council still exists :
In Beverley's circling mists !
Never loving our Coast ?
Of Wiv ne'er to boast ? ....
Rejection that persists.

*All* Streets are very eerie ;
No Public House how beery.
A Resort so hollow :
No Tourists will follow !
No laughter intense - or cheery.

The Fields, as well, are bare
[ No creatures grazing there ]
No farmyard bustle ;
No Auctions, no hustle ;
No wheat - but only tares.

Wiv sleeps now all through the year :
No signals of help to appear !
The Trains : they went first :
Sea's comeback much worse ?
That only leaves Place braced to Fear.

When an Ocean knows not its bounds -
When it logic and mercy confounds -
When a Town so diligently built
Is left to sadden and wilt :
We see raw Nature's power :
No bulb, no stem, no flower.

\*\*\*\*\*\*\*\*\*\*\*\*\*\*

PRINTED & BOUND BY WARD & PINKNEY [ PRINTERS ]
WEST 1, NORTHUMBERLAND AVENUE,
KINGSTON-UPON-HULL HU2 OLN
TEL: 01482 -325014